NORTHUMBERL

D0716886

Please return this book o ~~~~~~~~~ ed
below unless an extensio~~~ ~~ ~~an period is granted.

Application for renewal may be made by letter or telephone.

Fines at the approved rate will be charged when a book is
overdue.

Also published by Macmillan Children's Books

PANTS ON FIRE
Poems by Paul Cookson

A TWIST IN THE TALE
Poems chosen by Valerie Bloom

TRICK OR TREAT
Poems chosen by Paul Cookson

LOOK OUT!
the Teachers are Coming

Poems
chosen by

TONY
BRADMAN

illustrated by
MICHAEL
BROAD

MACMILLAN CHILDREN'S BOOKS

First published 2005 by Macmillan Children's Books
a division of Macmillan Publishers Limited
20 New Wharf Road, London N1 9RR
Basingstoke and Oxford
www.panmacmillan.com

Associated companies throughout the world

ISBN 0 330 43351 2

1 3 5 7 9 8 6 4 2

A CIP catalogue record for this book is available from
the British Library.

Printed and bound in Great Britain by Mackays of Chatham plc, Kent

Contents

The Lollipop Lady

Mrs Nadeem knows the street
And all the parents in their cars.
Dressed in yellow from chin to feet
    she's brighter than a thousand stars.

The world stops when she comes out.
Cars tremble, turn to stone.
Even soccer lads forget to shout
    when Mrs Nadeem walks alone.

Her lollipop held high, she towers
like a lighthouse while we beam
our happy way to school, and ours
    is a safe day, thanks to Mrs Nadeem.

Philip Burton

Days at School

Like any day
I open our front door.
Against the creosote fence,
Above the clustering pansies
The roses glow dull red;
And further off
Beyond the maple
And the overgrown canal
The orphan hill
That has no name
Rises to the blue.
Like every morning
I stand in the lay-by
In Penthryn Lane
Waiting for the bus.
Proudly Donna tells me,
'I'm going to Honey's house tonight.'
The brakes squeal.
Ann, the driver, wears a boiler suit
And works at Revill's garage in the town.
'Remind your mum
To leave me half a dozen eggs,'
She shouts her eyes upon the road ahead.
Because it's June and hot today
I sit with Kelly at the back
Beside an open window.
She's not my best friend
But you can always talk to her.
The wind that's blown across the Irish Sea
And half the breadth of Wales
Before rustling our homework books
And my brown hair

Smells hot this day of grass and tar.
Today we're up to Air and Light
In our Jam Jar Science Books.
Later we'll climb on the roof
To drop paper parachutes
On to the playing fields below.
Around the iron gates
The children shout and stare
As we get off the bus.
Next September I'll be at the High School
And someone else
Will sit in my place by the window.
There are stars that die each minute
Before their light comes down to us.
The bells rings
And we crowd shouting
Towards the shadows and the open door.

Gareth Owen

It's Busy in the Cloakroom (Under the Coats)

Darren's doing homework
   (late as usual)
Emma's brushing her hair
   (for the fifth time this morning)
Stevie's on his seventh Mars Bar
   (not as many as yesterday)
Derek's drinking fizzy pop
   (and saying the alphabet in burps)
Jasmin's trying to put as many Smarties as she can into her
     mouth
   (she's up to thirty-six and still smiling . . . just)
Barry's swapping football cards
   (same as every single playtime he's ever had)
Jayne is snogging Shaun
   (who's taken out his gum and put it on the peg for later)
Sunil, Leo and Zak are queuing behind Shaun
   (hoping to have a go before the bell rings)
Billy's making rude noises
   (but not with his mouth)
And Mr Little, the Headmaster, is crouching underneath an
     anorak
   (hiding from Mrs B, the school secretary)

Paul Cookson

First Day

Here in the great hall
Which smells of polish
The windows are so tall
And the floors so shiny
That everything feels funny
And not right at all
And I wish, I wish

That my sister was here,
That she was next to me,
That she was saying,
'Let's watch TV'
But that would be Home
And this is School
With everybody waiting

Until the music stops
And nobody talking
And me not knowing
Anybody, not anybody,
And all of us in lines
With teachers at the front
And sides, not smiling, looking

Worried and a bit cross
Then one of them
Is really friendly
With a big voice saying
Good morning, children
And everybody goes
Good morning, Mrs Someone.

And she has things
To tell us like it's someone's
Birthday, and I'm feeling
Better now, much
Better, and I look at the top
Of the tallest window
Where the sun is shining.

John Mole

Monday Assembly

Three hundred children
File into the hall,
Some of them are very big,
Some are very small.

Some of them are yawning,
Some are looking bright;
Some of them are black or brown,
Some of them are white.

Some of them are messy,
Some of them are neat;
Some are good at football,
Some have two left feet.

Some are very brainy,
And some always pass their tests;
Others find them very hard,
But try to do their best.

Some are very happy.
One or two are sad.
Most live with both parents,
Some with mum, or dad.

Some of them are dreaming
Of what they'd like to be;
Rich, or someone's best friend,
Or starring on TV.

Now the head is talking,
She's telling them what's what.
Some of them are listening,
Some of them are not.

And the head is saying
It's time to sing a hymn,
'All together, now!' she says.
'One, two, three – begin!'

All of them are singing
The hymn leads them along;
Three hundred voices
singing the same song.

Three hundred voices,
And each one is unique.
But they all blend together
As our school starts the week!

Tony Bradman

Mrs Blake and Miss Sharp

In Primary Four
we sat on the floor
and listened to stories with Mrs Blake.
We learned about bats
and Egyptian cats,
and how to make lemon and poppy seed cake.

She made us feel smart
and quite brilliant at art,
and never would laugh if we made a mistake.
The whole year went by
in the blink of an eye,
and she wished us all well in the summer break.

In Primary Five
we all must strive
to sit arrow-straight to please Miss Sharp.
She doesn't like noise,
(or girls, or boys)
and her mouth turns down like a scowling carp.

We do lots of sums
so whenever she comes,
our pencils must always be razor-sharp.
She tells us each day
what she wants us to say,
like Jack-and-the-Beanstalk's gold harp.

We hate Miss Sharp,
we loved Mrs Blake
It's amazing the difference a year can make.

Lynne Rickard

Childburst

It's playtime . . . it's childburst
and out they all run
Daniel slips over
and falls on his thumb.
Allison's fizzing
her ribbons aflame
Donna's a donkey
and Roger's a crane.
Cindy is squealing
and Cynthia skips
Marcus is laughing
and spitting out crisps.

Daren is fighting
and Emma's in tears
she's stuck in the railing
– right up to her ears.
Jacko is jumping
he's on Simon's back
his nose needs a wiping
his fingers are black
he's bellowing,
    yelling,
    pulling at hair
he knows how to fight
and he knows how to swear!
The puddle's in motion
it's splashing around
it's on Jacko's jacket
and Janice is drowned.
It's splashing and leaping
right up to the sky
it's on every nose
and it's in every eye.
The dustbins are shaking
they want to join in
they throw off their hats
and they dance to the din.
There's hidings
and seeking
    pushings
and squeals,
chasing of skirts
and dizzy cartwheels.

There's comics to flutter
to chase in the breeze
plasters in the cloakrooms
and scabs on the knees.
The gate is a palace,
this pebble a gem,
the step is a mountain,
the wall is a den . . .
Quick!
hide in the corner
but keep off the ground,
if your foot touches tarmac
you're bound to be found.
We'll scream and we'll bellow
we'll spit and we'll roar
hide in the toilets
and hold back the door.

Look!

Teachers are coming!
their thunderer blows
'stand with a partner
    walk in on your toes . . .'
Playtime is over
so walk back in twos
it's time for the telly
    and writing your news.

Peter Dixon

The Playground Dreams

I've lain here now for over fifty years;
in winter, puddles stand on my surface
or freeze into the cracks that summer left.
At night, I dream of hopscotch ladders
chalked on asphalt, the clatter
of small stones and thud
of children's feet. In my imagination,
multicoloured scooby-doos tangle
with cat's-cradle loops and spinning
hula hoops. There's a hint of gunpowder
from confiscated cap-guns, and a fizz
of sweet spilt sherbet. Ball bearings
jingle as ropes slap my tarmac
in condimented rhythm. Knicker elastic
twangs in memory and a red weal
blooms above white bobby socks.
Fivestones and jacks scratch
as they tumble and glass alleys
tickle as they roll. I can feel
an old taw lodged where I butt
against the annexe wall. Though
Four-eyes McPherson searched
the day it went astray,
and for a full week afterwards,
he never found it. I saw him cry
behind the bike shed,
but I'm no grass. I used to pretend
that I was the princess and it
was the pea that stopped my sleep;
now it soothes me to feel
the continuity. For fifty years
I've lain here, watching. All night

I dream scenes from the past until
the bleep of a Game Boy startles me
awake to the twenty-first century.

Gwyneth Box

Nature Study Sucks

Dear Lord provide us
With places to hide us
From long-legged spiders

And send us new teachers
Who don't show us leeches
And other such creatures

(I hate all those things and
I'm going to abscond
If I have to study
Another school pond)

Brian Patten

Bin There . . .

I start each school day smart and clean
A fresher bin you've never seen
But by day's end I've overflowed
With a squishy, squelching load

Today within my bag you'll find
Ink cartridges and orange rind
A scribbled note in secret code
A grubby plaster stained with blood

Squashed teabag from the teacher's cup
Spent drinks cans, crisp packs crumpled up
Banana skin covered in mould
Tuna sandwich, three days old.

Chewed spearmint gum, spat out in class
A stink bomb – little prankster's farce
A twelve-inch ruler snapped in two
Sweet wrappers, snot-covered tissue

Juice cartons, grubby bits of string
An apple, bruised and festering
Smudged spelling test, full of mistakes
A football that burst during break.

The cleaner grasps my bag of gunge
Wipes me with a soapy sponge
Squirts me with sweet-smelling spray
Ready for the next school day

Beverley Johnson

Fox

Midwinter, mid-morning
Of a dark-grey day.
Outside snow settles
On a playground
Where we won't be allowed to play.

We're inside, in the warm
Classroom, listening
As miss reads poems . . .
One where a fox
Comes trotting, green eyes glistening,

Out of a midnight forest,
Into a poet's mind.
I see it clearly:
Sharp ears, long snout,
Red, soft fur stirring in the wind . . .

The poem's called The Thought-Fox.
Miss says it's a great
Way of capturing
A fox in words.
Then I see it at the school gate,

There, where the bushes hide
Overflowing bins.
I hold my breath, stare
Through the window
And feel a tingling in my skin.

The fox breathes steam. It's real,
A city creature
Forced out in daylight
To scavenge scraps.
It stands proud, beyond our teacher.

'Miss!' someone hisses. 'It's
By the gate, just look!'
But miss keeps reading,
Takes no notice,
Eyes fixed on the pages of her book.

Whispers grow, till at last
Miss crossly turns, peers
Where we're all pointing,
But she's too late.
A swift red shadow disappears.

Miss tuts, and blames our strong
Imaginations,
The poem's power.
She looks away,
Happy with her explanation,

Picks up where she left off ...
But the trail is cold.
Outside snow settles,
Slowly covers
The tracks that show a fox was bold.

Tony Bradman

Cakes in the Staffroom

Nothing gets teachers more excited
than cakes in the staffroom at break time.
Nothing gets them more delighted
than the sight of plates
piled high with jammy doughnuts
or chocolate cake.

It's an absolute stampede
as the word gets round quickly,

And it's, 'Oooh these are really delicious,'
and, 'Aaah these doughnuts are ace.'

And you hear them say, 'I really shouldn't,'
or, 'Just a tiny bit, I'm on a diet.'

Really, it's the only time they're quiet
when they're cramming cakes into their mouths,

when they're wearing a creamy moustache,
or the jam squirts out like blood,
or they're licking chocolate
from their fingers.

You can tell when they've been scoffing,
they get languid in literacy,
sleepy in silent reading,
nonsensical in numeracy,
look guilty in assembly.

But nothing gets teachers more excited
than cakes in the staffroom at break time,
unless of course,
it's wine in the staffroom at lunchtime!

Brian Moses

I Am the Kid

I am the kid who says 'Break's over'
at exactly 10.44.
I am the kid whose job it is
to knock on the staffroom door.

We haven't drunk our coffees yet!
I wish you'd go away!
That child is such a pest!
are the sort of things they say.

They're never pleased to see me.
How the insults fly!
But I don't care if they're put out.
I love to hear them sigh.

I am the kid who says 'Time's up'.
The kid they don't adore.
Because I am the kid whose job it is
to knock on the staffroom door.

(And I am the kid
who's looking forward
to upsetting them again
at precisely 1.04.)

Bernard Young

Playtime

The playground is a lonely place
When you haven't got a friend
The seconds are all a minute long
And the minutes never end.

No one wants me to play
Or join in with their games
And if they speak to me at all
It's just to call me names.

I've tried standing by the teachers
But they soon send me away
And they always do it with the words
'Now off you go and play'.

So I slink off to a corner
And watch the others having fun
They're all in groups of two or more
But I am only one.

I don't know why no one likes me
Why I can't find a friend
All I know is that playtime
Just never seems to end.

Roger Hurn

Mrs Prince

Mrs Prince, from the office, is so kind,
Taking interest in our scabs. She doesn't mind
Blood, or bits of skin gone green.
And tenderly she smoothes on cream.
Mrs Prince says, 'Shall I ring up Mum or Dad?
I think that cut looks very bad.'
She has a tin of Smarties in her drawer.

That's what we fall over for.

Jacqueline King

Janitor's Cat

I sit in his room and stretch out my paws,
his chair I will use to sharpen my claws.

I'm fat and I'm happy, yet stripy and mean.
I sit and I wash till every bit's clean.

I rule the roost and I'm king of the hill
and I know that the children will all love me still.

With pats on the head and rubs on the chin,
and presents and titbits the kiddies bring in.

I sit and I sleep and dream dreams away.
There's always tomorrow to go out and play.

But till then I shall doze and peep out from one eye.
Yes, I've got it made till the day that I die.

Ian McInnes

Rainbow

Yesterday
my grandma said,
'There's all the colours of the rainbow
in your school.'

I knew that she was wrong.

We have no orange people,

nor green nor blue,

and you couldn't say
that Tony Wong was yellow,

more a pale and liquid gold
like corn ripening
under autumn sun.

You could say Ingrid
is close to white
with skin you can nearly see through;

Merle's is sleek and polished black,
lovely as a glossy plum,

but nobody is indigo or violet

I am the only one
that turns red on a sunny day,

but mostly I am pinkie grey
and so that doesn't count.

Today we went outside
measuring our playground.

'Give me your hand,' said Rashid.
Ahmed held his,
then Marita, Marvin, May Ling,
Yana, Zamato, Peter and the rest.

We found our playground is
exactly thirty children wide

and now we're working out
how many it would take
to go right round the earth.

We painted our own pictures
and our teacher put them on the wall.

Underneath she wrote:
**Friendship between children is like a
      rainbow.
It stretches right across our world.**

So after all my gran was right.

Barrie Wade

Lost Property Box

In our lost property box
there are socks with holes in
and shoes minus laces,
stand-up figures
without any bases,
a faded T-shirt
from Lanzarote,
a greatest-hits tape
by Pavarotti,
once champion conkers
shrunken with age,
a mystery book
without the last page,
sandwich boxes
with last month's bread in,
PE shorts
I wouldn't be seen dead in,
unloved toys and
mislaid gloves,
a Christmas card with
two turtle doves,
red underpants
decidedly manky,
a barely used
laced-edged hanky,
a love letter
from David Pratt
to his girlfriend Sally,
what about that!

And right at the bottom,
what I'm looking for,
the sports shirt I borrowed
from the boy next door ...

Perhaps he won't bash me
now I've found it!

Brian Moses

Elvin

For twenty-one days we'd turned the eggs –
now noughts, now crosses
(that's how we'd marked them),
and filled in the chart.

The infants came into our class
to see the incubator and learn
about hatching and stuff.
We promised to let them know.

Today, day twenty-two, Alan saw the crack.
We all took turns watching,
Jill and Jacqueline stayed in all playtime.
The crack got bigger.

While we were eating dinner, ravioli again,
and apple crumble with pink custard,
Elvin hatched out.
He was fluffy brown, not fluffy yellow.

We all stroked him.
It was lucky we called him 'him',
because later we found out
he would grow up to be a cockerel.

But actually we called him Elvin
because of Mrs Elvin, our caretaker,
who's great and doesn't mind mess at all.
Just as well, with all that straw and sawdust.

Catherine Benson

Our Teacher's Great

Our teacher's great.
She tells us stories and teaches us
songs with crazy noises.

Our teacher's great.
She let us sculpt with clay
and paint with jazzy
rainbow colours every day.

Our teacher's great.
She reads us poems with rhythm
that make us want to dance –
round the classroom,
in the playground,
all the way going home.

Our teacher's great.
She lets us bring our pets to school:
snakes, mice, my dog Ben
and Craig's terrapin April Fool.

Our teacher's great.
When someone broke my Prefect badge
and took the magnet off the back
she said, 'How do you feel about that?'
and listened while I told her
then made me another, just the same.

Joan Poulson

Our School's Firework Night

We exploded into the playground
Fizzing with excitement
Spinning and crackling with laughter
Twirling our torches to write our names
On the November air.

Little brothers stood at the front,
Bundled and muffled in zipped warmth.
Little sisters spiralled like smoke
Around their mothers' skirts.

The countdown began.

Across the field we saw the first spark
Dart down to touch the poised row of rockets.
We held our ears
Dreading and longing for
The Big Scream,

And the rain started.
Gentle for a while,
Spitting, teasing, frizzing our hair,
Staining our shoulders
Until the babies began to wail.
Then faster and harder,
Soaking our shoes,
Sending cold streams of misery
Down our collars
Down our upturned faces.

The crowd bloomed with umbrellas
As the far-off fathers ran with smouldering fuses
To light the lovely displays.
Catherine Wheels that twisted off their sticks,
Fiery Flowers that wilted and drooped
Against the gloomy sky,
Mighty Atoms that popped like paper bags,
Volcano Mountains that erupted with choking green fog,
And a final, forlorn message
To send us home.
'___OD __IG__.'

'Goodnight,' we called sadly
As we trailed away
Like squibs.
'Od ig.
Od ig.'

Clare Bevan

Wet Playtime

The window's blurred with rain,
Outside it pelts and pours,
The playground's one big pimpled puddle.
Sir goes for morning tea,
Says, 'Settle down indoors,
Behave yourselves, don't make a muddle.'
So what do we do to keep off the gloom
On a rotten wet day shut up in our room?
Well, Neville has always been curious to know:
Can he scratch his left ear with his right foot big toe?
So he's trying it now, while Jonathan Rose
Is making his pen disappear up his nose.
The Robinson twins (nicknamed Big-Ears and Noddy)
Are giggling over a book called *Your Body*,
And Hannah's got chalk and is drawing – good Lord! –
A horrible picture of Sir on the board.
There's a buzz from some kids who are racing the snails:
Flash leading but Fred's coming up on the rails;
There's a battleship bombing across at the sink –
The water's about to slop over, I think –
Ooh yes, now it has and it's all pouring through
To the cupboard where Sir keeps spare rolls for the loo;
And now, would you believe it, some great clumsy ox
Has spilt powder paint in the dressing-up box!
And the rest of the class? Well, I won't spell it out,
But the rest of the kids are mucking about ...

'Sir's coming!'
We all rush at no end of a rate
To hide all things wet, bent or bust,
And we're all reading nicely,
And Sir says, 'That's great,
I see you're a class I can trust.'

Eric Finney

Classroom

Classrooms are creatures
a kind of pet,
some are naturally sunny
others a bit gloomy
but it's how we look after them
that makes the difference in how they feel

day after day, week after week
we leave the print of our presence
without scratching names in wood
or a scribble of felt-tip pens
the room absorbs
the touch of our hands, elbows, feet
the smell of our fear, the sound of our laughter,
marks the cleaners cannot remove
the ghost stains of growing lives
built up class after class year after year

it is because of this
that a classroom with no one in it
is emptier than other empty rooms
it waits with the sad uncertain manner of a dog
left in a car or tied outside a shop –
when we go in at a weekend or worse on holidays
when the chairs stand on the desks
and the dust rests calmly, unafraid of cleaners,
the room seems in a troubled sleep, a fretful
hibernation,
as if it remembers it has a purpose but
has forgotten who it is without its children

Dave Calder

My Desk

I like my desk when the sun slides in
and warms the ink inside my pen.

I like my desk and its thunderclap
and its silences and its tap tap tap.

I like my desk for its woody smell,
its heron legs that ring-a-ding-bell.

I like my desk at reading hour
snug with my book like a bee in a flower.

I like my desk so flat and wide
to rest my picture and paints astride.

I like my desk when home time's near.
I whisper, Thank you desk, my dear.

Philip Burton

According to Our Caretaker...

I am not here to find lost property
Or to empty the bins or to clean graffiti...

I am not here to be called from my bed
To free from the railings some idiot's head...

I am not here to sweep up the yard,
To clean dirty windows or act as your guard...

I am not here cos some nincompoop's locked
In a kit cupboard or cos some drain's blocked...

AND I am not here to retrieve the ball
That YOU – careless brat – just kicked over the wall...

The reason I'm here – pay attention BIGSHOT –
Is to...? Let me think... Oh dear me... I've forgot!

Philip Waddell

Our Dinner Lady

Mrs Osman is scarlet
   and thin as a drinking straw.
She's fizzy inside
   and tells jokes about spam
and what her gran did in the war.

She bends towards you
(if you're naughty and chew with mouth open wide)
and she sings, 'Tiptoe through the two-lips
through the two-lips, if you'll pardon me?'

She picks up your fork
to prod your oven potato and serenade it,
   'Spud, spud, glorious spud –
nothing quite like it for
   cooling the blood!'

Carry on eating to stop her
(with two lips tight when you chew).

I sing her songs in the corridor
and practise her jokes in the yard.
'With a little bit of this, and a little bit of that
we fill your plate da da da da!'

Philip Burton

Donkeys and Stars

It's dress-rehearsal day for the Nativity.
Reception are trying on their costumes.
There are uniforms draped like skins over desks.
There are donkeys and stars in the classroom.

Jamie has lost his ears and nose.
Ibrahim's tights are all wonky.
Natasha's forgotten her sparkly shoes.
Thomas is pulling the tail off a donkey.

Miss Fowler wants the stars on stage right now.
That's Darren and Aaron and Zoe and Jess.
Three of the stars are ready to shine.
Aaron has his head up Mary's dress.

The donkeys are starting their journey,
Carrying their tails so they don't trip over.
They plod their way to the stable scene,
Through a swishing, swirling supernova.

It's dress-rehearsal day for the Nativity.
Reception are on stage in their costumes.
There is silence, stillness, a heavenly peace,
Where there were donkeys and stars in the classroom.

Alan Durant

The Winter Display

For the winter display we write poems
of the wintry wolf's lonely call –
we paint frosty fields,
turquoise skies, spindly trees,
and it all goes up on the wall.

Then every year in December
we begin on the Christmas caper,
making stars and snowflakes
from hexagonal shapes
and use up all the school's gold paper.

We stare out of our classroom window
at the freezing fog or the storm,
and as the school corridors
fill up with work,
we are happy to be in the warm.

But when the summer display comes along
and we're drawing blue skies and crayoning them,
who wants to paint pictures
of sunny green fields?
We'd rather be outside
playing in them.

Roger Stevens

Playground in Winter

Beneath our feet
The snow crunches
And bunches together
At the side of the playground,
Where the caretaker has tried shovelling it
Once he'd decided
Snow 'would look better' tidied.

Now, what remains
Of one earlier
'Icy' slide
Takes a visitor to the school
On an 'unexpected' ride.

We watch, as she struggles
To stand upright again.

The end of playtime.

A whistle's blow –
And we enter,
Leaving our footprint pools
To slowly change
Into a blackened sludge
The length of the corridors.

Trevor Harvey

About Mrs Barry, by Sarah

Mrs Barry sits enthroned
On her royal blue Teaching Chair
Her robe is a fuzzy pink cardigan
Her crown is her silver hair
And a smile and a twinkle light up the wrinkles
In her soft and comfortable skin
As she says,
'Well now, my fine little ladies and gentlemen,
Shall we begin?'

Mrs Barry taught my mother
In olden days when she was young
Taught her how to sit correctly
When to speak, or hold her tongue
And I picture my mum as a little girl
Seeing that twinkling grin
And hearing,
'Well now, my fine little ladies and gentlemen,
Shall we begin?'

And when Earth's last generation
Lives under a dying sun
And the final class of humanity's children
Silvery-suited, one by one
Arrive before their teacher,
She'll smile as they all troop in
And say,
'Well now, my fine little ladies and gentlemen,
Shall we begin?'

John Dougherty

School Midnight

The bell rings, and it's school midnight.
Here's Mr Pettifer, pompous and plump
and Mr Jason, lean and looming
and Miss Fairless, with hairs on her chin.
They keep their canes in a cupboard in the corner
not just for use, they say, but as a warning.

First, second and third head teachers,
they made our school and they made the rules.
At school midnight, when the bell rings
they step out together, plump Mr Pettifer
arm in arm with stern Mr Jason
and Fanny Fairless, who sees everything.

1890 to 1897: that was Mr Pettifer's time.
1897 to 1910: that was Miss Fairless's time.
1910 until he'd been there forever
(or at least as long as anyone could remember)
long-lived and lean and looming:
Mr Jason.

The bell rings, and here they come
down the corridors, into the classrooms
with a sweep of skirts and a rattle of watch chains,
running their fingers over the shelves for dust,
scanning our handwriting, opening books,
checking the registers, noting the absences . . .

The bell rings, and it's school midnight.
Miss Fairless is standing by the piano
waiting sternly for absolute quiet.
Mr Pettifer puts his hands together
while Mr Jason strides down the aisle
between ghostly rows of whispering children
who laugh when he shows them the cane.

Helen Dunmore

The Old Boiler

Conditions here are arctic
We're sitting in our coats
Miss has got the sniffles
We've all got sore throats

Annually it happens
Every winter it's the same
The temperature's sub-zero
And the boiler is to blame

Thanks to the boiler
We all freeze
Thanks to the boiler
Our lessons cease

And we have to be sent home at lunchtime
What a shame!

Thanks to the boiler
Long may it rule
Thanks to the boiler
Our boiler's really cool!

Bernard Young

Drawer

Don't open Miss MacDonald's drawer
or put your hand inside to get
your confiscated lollipop
catapult or cyberpet.

Behind our toys, the broken chalk,
snapped pencils and bent paper clips
something strange lurks in the dark –
we're just not sure of what it is.

We've seen Miss slip in crumbs and crusts,
orange peel and apple cores,
we've heard low growls, soft thumping and
the scritch-scratch of sharp tiny claws.

But when we ask her what it is,
Miss smiles – 'It's a dinosaur:
don't you believe me? Keep your fingers out
– my pet likes to eat them raw.'

Dave Calder

New Girl

When we moved house to these parts late last year
And had to find a school midterm, I started here.
The main thing I remember is the fear.
'Don't make a fuss,' Mum said.

It was akin to falling in the sea:
Classrooms brimful of cold hostility.
Lips moved, but not aloud – inaudibly.
Hard to catch my breath,
Way beyond my depth:
Drowning.
And when I looked around, all I could see
Were circling sharks baring their teeth at me.

A new girl started school with us today:
A skinny waif with nothing much to say
Who cried and said she didn't want to stay

'OK by us,' I said.

And Miss was going to make her sit by me
Until I said I had an allergy
To ginger girls whose surnames started with G.,
Stinking garlic breath,
Faces white as death:
Frowning.
At break we joked – not wishing to alarm her –
That we feed new girls to the school piranha.

Geraldine McCaughrean

Still

Head up,
in the middle of a test,
the room is as still
as my nan's display
of best china.

The raised lettering
on a clean jam jar
catches a fragment
of sunlight and sparkles briefly.

On a dusty window ledge
a straggling buttercup
in an old milk bottle
trails its spindly roots
into a thin coin
of dead water.

Someone coughs.
A single yellow petal falls.
No one notices.

Head down,
I turn the page.

Bob Shannon

Parents' Evening

Hello, Mrs Spinner
Now, about your son, Sam

First of all I must say
I'm sorry to hear about your Rottweiler
Sam says it's been poorly
Well, the number of times it's eaten Sam's homework
I'm not surprised.
And then it gave Sam dog-flu and he was away
On the day that Brighton played Spurs in the cup
And it was a shame that it chewed Sam's PE kit
What's that?
You don't have a Rottweiler?
You don't even have a dog?
How strange.

By the way, Mrs Spinner,
May I congratulate your husband
On being chosen to represent England
In the next Olympics.
You must be very proud.
He's a shot-putter, Sam says.
And Sammy tells me you're a model.
And you're in those bra commercials.
What's that?
You have to be going?

You have something to say to Sammy?
Well, lovely to meet you at last.
Tell Sammy I'm looking forward
To seeing him tomorrow.

Goodbye, Mrs Spinner.
Goodbye.

Roger Stevens

Every Night
Mr Miller Dreams

Every night Mr Miller dreams
of the day he will retire.
There'll be a small party
in the staffroom
during the lunch hour
and at final assembly
he'll receive a major gift
from the whole school
plus presents
from individual pupils
who will be heartbroken
to see him leave.
Children, past and present
(some now grown up),
will file past to thank him
for being so inspirational
– for changing their lives.

In the evening
a large group of colleagues and friends
will take him out for drinks
and a meal.
There will be speeches
charting his impressive career
and praising his achievements.

He can't wait.

Day two. Week one. First job.
A long way to go.

Every night Mr Miller dreams.

Bernard Young

The Staffroom

When we go outside,
In the cold, or the hot,
Or whatever weather we've got,
They go in. Miss Daniels, Mrs Cooper,
Mr Wallaby, Mrs Roper,
Miss Fletcher, Miss Harding,
Mr Spall, Mrs Henry, and Miss Evans,
All of them, in.

Into a room that is not very big,
With only nine chairs, and a kettle,
And close the door.
'Put the kettle on!'
Well, well. What happens in there?
Because out of thin air come
Nancy and Rita and Eric and Pearl,
Justine and Mary, John, Susan and Shirl.

They laugh and they chatter and make such a din,
Till the bell rings for lessons, and then they begin
To come out of the room that I've only peeked in.
Miss Daniels, Mrs Cooper,
Mr Wallaby, Mrs Roper,
Miss Fletcher, Miss Harding,
Mr Spall, Mrs Henry, and Miss Evans.
But where are the others? They never appear
Until the next time someone says,
'I'll put the kettle on.'

Margaret Carey

The School Doctor

When the school doctor came there were lots of rumours
that she takes a pint of blood to see if you've got tumours.
And pokes down your ear and sometimes finds some ants.
And she tells you to strip off right the way down to your pants.
And she gives you injections in the foot and the knee.
And puts eye drops in your eyes so you can hardly see.
And she looks in your hair to find nits and fleas and lice.
And her fingers are pointy and feel as cold as ice.

Then when I went, it wasn't like that all.
I just had to read some big letters on the wall.
And she listened to my back and shone a torch in my ear,
and rattled different things to see if I could hear.
Then she laughed and said, 'Now, this is my favourite bit!'
and tapped me on the leg with a stick that made me kick.
She was quite funny, and she didn't have cold hands.
(BUT I DID HAVE TO STRIP OFF RIGHT THE WAY
DOWN TO MY PANTS.)

Sean Taylor

School Si ns

They've had signs up all over our school
to name all the places; I don't know why
because we already know where everything is.
Anyway, someone, who won't put their hand up,
has been picking off letters; they come off
like sticky labels on bottles come off
only a bit harder.
The LOWER PLAYGROUND
is now LOVER LAY ROUND,
the boys' loos say BOY TO LET and
Bob's workshop now says CAR TAKER.
I like Bob.
At 12.30 we all line up and walk in the
DIN   HALL, which Mrs Maderson, our head,
who is very furious about it all, said was
'actually rather 'propriate', and
Mrs Geoffrey, the secretary, now works in the
SECRET   OF ICE, which I think
sounds dead mysterious.
Then there are the ASSROOMS,
which is a swearing word really and
HEAD ACHE and
DEPUTY HEAD ACHE,
which my dad thinks is brilliant and says that
it would have been HEAD STRESS in his day
except that the signs would have been hand-painted
by someone called a sign-writer,
and you couldn't pick the letters off.

Trevor Parsons

Out of Class

It was that last half hour in the morning –
Coming up to dinner time and I was trying
To finish my 'five sentences about myself'

And I couldn't remember how many Rs in 'embarrassed'
And when Miss Lyon sent me to the Secretary
With the Games List I was quite pleased because

You can duck into the Library and ask Mrs Hofmann.
Although she's German she can spell any English world
Better than anybody. Year Four were watching telly in
   Resources

And there was a boy standing outside Mr Devon's room,
Like always. Sometimes there are two, one each side
Of the door. He won't let them stand together.

When I went through the Lower Hall the ladies
Were putting the tables out and joking to each other
And one of them dropped a tray full of knives and forks

With a crash and said something not very ladylike.
I pretended not to hear. The piano was open and someone
Had drawn a cartoon face on the board; and year three

Had left the recorders all anyhow on the stage blocks.
I knocked on the Office door and the new Secretary
With the bright red nails just took the list off me

Without looking at me. There was that smell of stew.
I heard Mrs Foyle shouting so I went back via the toilets.
As soon as I picked up my pen I realized I'd forgotten

To ask Mrs Hofmann, so I guessed and put in two Rs
And that turned out to be right (Exclamation Mark!)
But I missed out one of the esses. Just my luck.

Then Miss Docherty next door must have let hers out early
Because you could hear them all squealing in the corridor.
And then little Simon Orimbo came round ringing the bell.

Gerard Benson

Summer Fête

It's dashing here, and dashing there,
It's heaps of boxes, tables, chairs.
It's looping flags and testing speakers,
Hyped-up children, frazzled teachers.

Welly wanging, Zap the Rat,
Pin the Whiskers on the Cat.
Hoopla, apple dunking, darts,
'Karaoke Korner' stars.

Stalls for cakes and sweets and bottles,
Knick-knacks, toys, old books and comics.
Piping hot dogs, bacon baps,
Cups of tea and ginger snaps.

Dinner ladies on the march
Selling raffle tickets hard.
'Cornetto Man' is Mr Tilly,
Mrs Moor is Gipsy Lily.

Bouncy castle, Whack the Hammer,
Skittles, pony rides, the clamour
Round the big tombola barrel,
Shoot the arrow at King Harold.

Hey, the Head is in the stocks
In his bathing trunks and socks
Grab your sponge, all slopping wet.

SPLOSH!

Terrific! Best game yet!

Patricia Leighton

Sports Day

Just four more days
so long to wait
till egg-and-spoon
and ball-and-plate,
till starting guns
and lightning starts
and pumping legs
and pounding hearts,
the thrilling chase
of every race,
the cooling breeze
upon my face,
the final push
so well rehearsed,
the burning drive
to come in first!
And there it is,
the finish line,
I'm almost through,
the prize is mine!
To top it all,
the races done,
it's time for ice cream,
games and fun.
Another year
of work and play
ends with a bang –
I love Sports Day!

Four days to go!
I count with dread,
each night
as I get into bed.

I've got to go,
there's no way out,
find something else
to think about
before a nightmare
starts to hatch,
with flying balls
I cannot catch,
and tripping shoes
with tangled laces,
pointing fingers,
laughing faces,
hoops and beanbags
zooming past,
always, always
coming last,
coming last.
No amount of
sporting fun
will make this day
a better one.
If only I
could sneak away
and read a book –
I hate Sports Day!

Lynne Rickard

Class Photograph

Everyone's smiling, grinning, beaming,
Even Clare Biggs who was really scheming
How she was going to get revenge
On her ex-best friend, Selina Penge
(Front row, third left, with hair in wisps)
For stealing her salt and vinegar crisps.

And Martin Layton-Smith is beaming,
Though he was almost certainly dreaming
Of warlock warriors in dripping caves
Sending mindless orcs to their gruesome graves.
(Next to him, Christopher Jordan's dream
Has got something to do with a football team.)

And Ann-Marie Struthers is sort of beaming
Though a minute ago her eyes were streaming
Because she'd been put in the second back row
And separated from Jennifer Snow,
And Jennifer Snow is beaming too
Though Miss Bell wouldn't let her go to the loo.

And Miss Bell, yes even Miss Bell, is beaming
Though only just now we'd heard her screaming
At the boy beside her, Robert Black,
Who kept on peeling his eyelids back
And making a silly hooting noise
(Though he said that was one of the other boys).

Eve Rice is doing her best at beaming.
Yes, Eve is reasonably cheerful-seeming
Though I think she was jealous because Ruth Chubb
Had – at last! – let me into their special club.
(In order to join this club, said Ruth,
You had to have lost at least one tooth.)

And look, there's me, and my teeth are gleaming
Around my new gap; yes, I'm really beaming.

Julia Donaldson

There Are Giants in My School

Who stride along with their heads in the sky
And thunder across the wide playground
Rumbling and roaring through the doors
To stretch in vast treelines
On big assembly chairs
Bellowing for dinner
Frowning down like
Frost or smiling like
End of term
On me
And I
Stare
Up and fix
My gaze upon
Their bigness and
Wonder how I will
Ever be a giant in Year Six

Addy Farmer

Nice Miss Jones

Last year I had to join Year One,
And soon I'll start Year Three,
But now I'm in nice Miss Jones's class
And THAT'S the place for me.

Don't want to start Year One again
(They sniff and suck their thumbs).
Don't want to be a Junior
(They have to do hard sums).

Don't want to swap Miss Jones's room,
It's safe in here and cosy.
Don't want another teacher who
Is cross and strict and nosy.

Don't want to leave the Infants' School.
Don't want to grow up clever.
Just want to stay with kind Miss Jones
And be in Year Two FOREVER.

Clare Bevan

School Report

Jason is

No good at Maths:
sticky with numbers,
can't count for toffee.

As for English:
he is very good
at Games!

His spelling
is magic –
i.e.
mumbo jumbo!

His History is
a thing of the past,
here today
and gone tomorrow.

His Geography is
sadly
all over the place.

I draw the line
at his Drawing:
the only conclusion
to be drawn is
you wouldn't pin up
his pin-ups!

When he was
Nature Table Monitor
(briefly)
this year

The frogspawn
turned purple
and the gerbil asked
could it go
into Class Three.

Jason needs
a brain transplant,
his mouth washing out
(ears too),

Needs de-footballing,
unscrewing
and putting back together
properly again,

A good dose of
the Encyclopaedia Britannica
three times a day.

His teachers think
he is trying.

Yes! Very!

Matt Simpson

Teachers' Awards

At the end of each summer term
    amid much jollity and backslapping,
schoolteachers congratulate each other
    on surviving yet another school year.

So let's hear it for Mrs King,
    the queen of the big production number,
always on a short fuse,
    especially on duty days.

And not forgetting . . . Mr White
    for staying calm when the classroom radiator
leaked rusty water all over
    his recently completed pile of report cards.

Let's hear it for . . . Mrs Salmon,
    who restrained herself quite admirably
when the school gerbil
    ate her winning lottery ticket.

And for Mr Middleton, who has eaten school dinners
    for each day of his twenty-year career,
unable to be with us tonight,
    but we hope he'll be out of hospital soon.

And the romance of the year award
    goes to Miss Buchanan and Mr Duke,
they're dreadfully drippy when they're together,
    it really makes us . . . feel unwell!

And last of all, our dear headmaster,
    who led us all through good times and bad,
till our school inspection came along
    and he suddenly discovered
        a pressing engagement in Barbados.

So let's hear it for those
    fabulous, wonderful creatures,
where would you be without them?
    Let's hear it for THE TEACHERS . . .

Brian Moses

Going Home Time

Mummies and daddies at the gate
Turn up early and enjoy the wait.
Babies in pushchairs, toddlers round their feet
They find this a happening place to meet.
My mum is there among the rest.
She thinks she's doing it for the best.

I fix her with an angry glare.
She returns my look with a steady stare.
I make a quick dash to the other gate
I can't walk with her, I've promised my mate.
We walk back to his, I can phone her when
I think she's had time to get home with Ben.

Doesn't she know that I'm old enough now?
Can't she tell she shames me and how
My mates will tease, can't stand much more?
I want to go home alone now I'm in Year Four.

Pamela Brown

Life After School

The school bell has rung and the children are gone,
But life in the classroom still goes on.

At the back of the cupboard, a little brown mouse
Has found a most suitable place for a house.
Her tiny, sharp teeth efficiently shred
Paper and tissue to soften her bed.

Through a narrow gap in the wooden floor,
A woodlouse has come for his evening explore.
A moth at the window is trying in vain
To fly to the moon through a crack in the pane.

And, taking some exercise after his meal,
Hammy the hamster is running the wheel.
(During the daytime when children come peeping,
Hammy the hamster is curled up sleeping.)

The beans that were planted in yogurt-pot beds
Are starting to sprout and push up their heads.
A snail has escaped and is munching his way
Through a vase of sweet peas on the nature display.

A leftover sandwich, cheesy and old,
Is growing some rather disgusting blue mould.
In a tank full of compost, industrious worms
Excavate tunnels with wriggles and squirms.

And skilfully labouring overhead,
A spider is spinning her silken thread.
Setting a trap from the clock to the light,
To capture her innocent prey-midflight.

Yes, the school bell has rung and the children are gone
But life in the classroom still goes on.

Doda Smith

Last Day

This class was special.

No one was particularly clever,
Particularly naughty,
Particularly messy,
Particularly anything.

Nothing miraculous happened,
Nothing stunning,
Or funny, or frightening, or strange.

Each day was much like another
As the year crept softly by,
Leaving its ordinary debris
Of drawings and stories
And small successes
And unremarkable memories.

Yet something hung between us,
Something that glittered like chalk dust
On a sunny day.

It was nothing you could touch,
Or capture,
Or exactly define,
But when I see the scattered offerings
Left on my desk –
A necklace of shells,

A giant pot of talcum
Smelling of yesterday,
A limp bunch of yellow flowers,
A crumpled card
Signed with love –
I can hardly bear
To walk away.

This class was special.

Clare Bevan

Carry On Not Carrying On

I'm sick of books and pens,
don't like carrying them round,
all day and every day.

Forget projects and files,
bulky and awkward,
just get in the way.

Don't like pencil cases and rulers,
all angular and sharp.

As for that PE kit,
I hate lugging that around . . .
socks and trainers that smell like mouldy cheese
and a shirt that hasn't been washed since last month.

The lunch box is a pain too.
Keeps coming open.
I can't stand the smell of egg sandwiches
and I hate it when the orange juice leaks,
the chocolate biscuits melt
and I end up sticky and gooey.

No, I can't be doing with all this carry-on.
I'm looking forward to a rest.
No school for six weeks
I just want to be left alone to relax a bit.

Mind you, I hope I get emptied and tidied this year.

Last Summer I was stuck with everything for six weeks.
Horrible it was.
Disgusting!
Books, pens, files and projects,
pencil cases, rulers, smelly kit, leaky lunch boxes,
orange cartons, biscuits wrappers . . .

it's no fun being a school bag, I can tell you.

Paul Cookson

One Small School Ghost

It was only a small ghost
and did no harm at all.
At least, that's what those
who knew it always said.

You could hear it sometimes
singing to itself
behind the hall curtains,
hopscotching down a corridor,
whistling tunes
out of cloakroom taps.

It played jungle swings
among the anoraks,
tip-and-catch with dropped pencils,
one-a-side football
with abandoned Pepsi cans.
It had a whale of a time.

Sometimes it sat in on lessons.
If you were lucky,
it sat next to you.
Those were the times sums
magically came out right,
words flowed from nowhere.

The teachers knew it was there.
They'd stare into spaces,
smile oddly at desks, open doors.
Some even christened it!
James . . . Freddy . . . Alfonso,
their own pet names.

The cleaners, too, knew more
than they were telling.
Not that they were scared,
not a bit of it;
called it their 'little lovey',
left it chocolate drops.

It was a small ghost, a happy ghost,
until the workmen came . . .

Then walls were knocked down,
classrooms changed,
new blocks built and,
whether it was the smell of paint,
the newness or all the turmoil,
the ghost left.

We sensed it as soon
as we walked in for the new term,
sensed it wherever we went.
In Final Assembly that day,
the head gushed: new classrooms,
more space, more pupils.

But those in the know
silently ticked
one small ghost
off the school roll.
There was something else
new around school

– an emptiness.

Patricia Leighton

A selected list of titles available from
Macmillan Children's Books

Pants on Fire	Poems by Paul Cookson	0 330 41798 3	£3.99
A Twist in the Tale	Poems chosen by Valerie Bloom	0 330 39899 7	£3.99
Trick or Treat	Poems chosen by Paul Cookson	0 330 42630 3	£3.99

All Pan Macmillan titles can be ordered from our website,
www.panmacmillan.com, or from your local bookshop
and are also available by post from:

**Bookpost,
PO Box 29, Douglas, Isle of Man IM99 1BQ**

Credit cards accepted. For details:
Telephone: 01624 677237
Fax: 01624 670923
Email: bookshop@enterprise.net
www.bookpost.co.uk

Free postage and packing in the United Kingdom